Winter Solstice Wish

by **KATE ALLEN FOX**

illustrated by **ELISA PAGANELLI**

beaming ☀ books
MINNEAPOLIS

For Mom and Dad, who were always there —**KAF**
To Miranda, my sunbeam in every day —**EP**

Library of Congress Cataloging-in-Publication Data

Names: Fox, Kate Allen, author. | Paganelli, Elisa, illustrator.
Title: Winter solstice wish / by Kate Allen Fox ; illustrated by Elisa
  Paganelli.
Description: Minneapolis, MN : Beaming Books, 2024. | Audience: Ages 3-8. |
  Summary: On the shortest day of the year, communities come together to
  celebrate and savor every ray of light.
Identifiers: LCCN 2023046905 (print) | LCCN 2023046906 (ebook) | ISBN
  9781506492858 (hardback) | ISBN 9798889830641 (ebook)
Subjects: CYAC: Winter solstice--Fiction. | Belonging--Fiction. | LCGFT:
  Picture books.
Classification: LCC PZ7.1.F69135 Wi 2024 (print) | LCC PZ7.1.F69135
  (ebook) | DDC [E]--dc23
LC record available at https://lccn.loc.gov/2023046905
LC ebook record available at https://lccn.loc.gov/2023046906

30 29 28 27 26 25 24   1 2 3 4 5 6 7 8 9

Hardcover ISBN: 978-1-5064-9285-8
eBook ISBN: 979-8-8898-3064-1

Beaming Books
PO Box 1209
Minneapolis, MN 55440-1209
Beamingbooks.com

Printed in China.

In the shortest days of winter,
when golden light disappears
faster than a steaming cup of cocoa,
we savor every drop of sunshine.

We slurp down every moment,
knowing that dusk soon lurks.

This time of year,
when our half of the planet tips
farther and farther from the sun,

we pass more and more hours in
shadow,
        cold,
            night . . .

until *today*—the winter solstice.
The shortest day of the year.

Today we stretch the daylight
as much as we can, trying to make it last.

We beachcomb and build castles,
grains of sand slipping slyly
through our hands.

As the last fingers of sunlight
stretch above the horizon—
shrinking with each minute—

we unpack our firewood,
piling piece after piece,
collecting them like
candles for wishing.

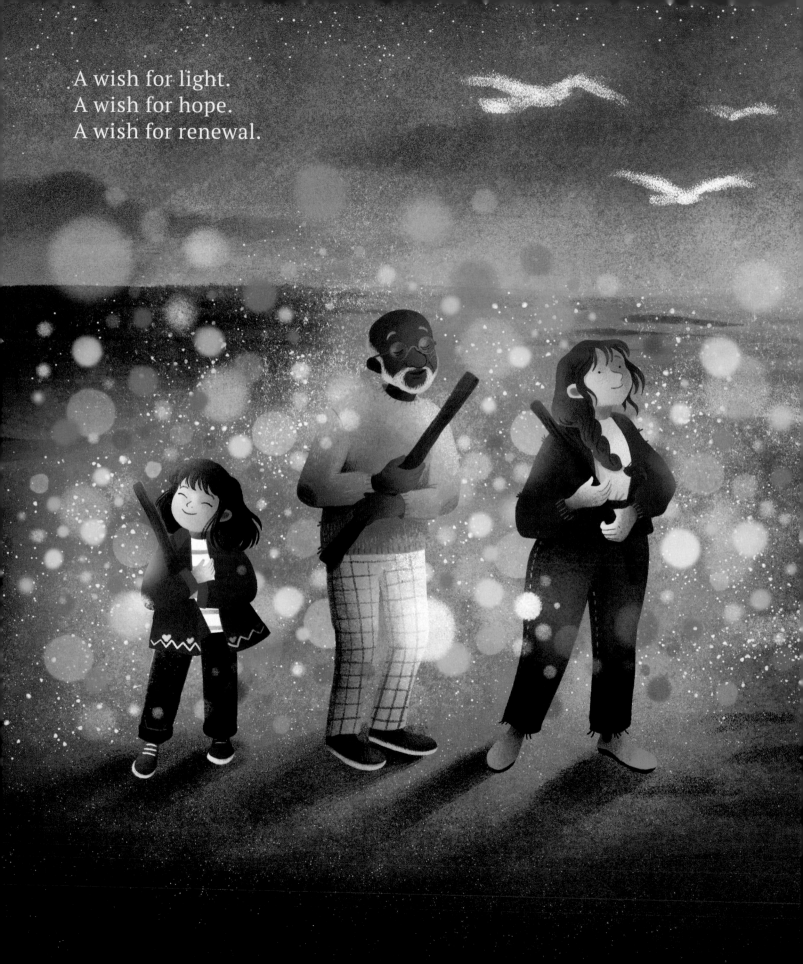

A wish for light.
A wish for hope.
A wish for renewal.

Wish by wish,
our pile grows until . . .

the day slips away.

Night
    surrounds,
        envelops,
            embraces.

So we search for the light.

When fear prickles our skin,
our hands reach for one another,
squeezing in silent reassurance.

A reminder:
I am still here.
A promise:
I always will be.

Then, a match
flicks,
flashes,
whooshes
to life.
Flame by tiny flame,

the heat grows,
building into a blaze.
The amber flames

lick the sky,
savoring the star-speckled night.

Light reflects off the sand,
creating an orb for us alone.

We sit
    in the glow,
    in the heat,
    in the aura
of wishes grown large,
of the light we built together.

Around the globe,
other hands reach out,

holding hope,
holding space,
holding one another.

Hands that span
to the far side of the globe,
where others bask in a solstice of their own—

the *longest* day of their year.

Here, we rest easy,
knowing that our side of the earth will,
little by little, tilt back toward the sun.

That tomorrow daylight will return.
That it will grow and grow,
minute by minute,
day after day.

And that we will savor every drop.
Together.

AUTHOR'S NOTE

This story is inspired by winter solstice beach bonfires that sometimes take place near my home in San Diego, California. Over a thousand years ago in northern Europe, the Norse people marked the darkest time of year with large bonfires to scare off evil spirits and encourage the light to return.

WINTER SOLSTICE CELEBRATIONS

This Norse tradition still inspires many solstice celebrations and is incorporated into St. Lucia's Day, which is celebrated in Scandinavian countries on December 13. But there are many other solstice traditions around the world. In ancient Rome, the festival of Saturnalia occurred around the time of the solstice and included games and gift-giving. Many elements of Saturnalia were later incorporated into Christmas and New Year celebrations. In China, the Dongzhi festival, which also began thousands of years ago, is celebrated with special foods, including rice balls called *tang yuan*.

The winter solstice is also celebrated in Peru, Iran, and even Antarctica, among many other places. While we all experience the solstice in different ways depending on where we live, everyone can celebrate the idea of hope on the shortest day of the year.

WHAT IS A SOLSTICE?

The earth tilts on its axis. When your part of the planet is closer to the sun, you will feel warmer. When it tilts farther away, you will feel colder. This is what makes seasons change. It also changes how many hours of sunlight you see each day. When your part of the planet is tilted the farthest away from the sun, you will see the least amount of sunlight. This is called the winter solstice—the shortest day of the year.

THE TWO SOLSTICES

When you are experiencing the winter solstice, people on the other side of the planet are experiencing the summer solstice—the longest day of the year. This makes sense because when one half of the planet is tipped away from the sun, the other half must be closer to the sun. Imagine a teeter-totter: when one side goes up, the other must go down. It's *kinda* like that.

In the northern hemisphere, people experience the winter solstice on December 20 or 21. That is the summer solstice in the southern hemisphere. And the northern hemisphere experiences the summer solstice (the longest day of the year) on June 20 or 21. This is the winter solstice in the southern hemisphere.

SAFETY FIRST!
Beach fires should only be built by adults and enjoyed with adult supervision. With an adult, check your local laws to understand where fires can be built in your area. Always use a designated fire pit.

KATE ALLEN FOX is the author of *Pando: The Living Wonder of Trees* and *A Few Beautiful Minutes: Experiencing a Solar Eclipse*. After working in public health, she combined her passions for science and the written word and began writing inspiring nature-based picture books. She lives, hikes, and homeschools in California with her family.

ELISA PAGANELLI was born in Italy. After completing artistic studies, she made a career in advertising and has been the founder of a small award-winning design/trade business. She now lives and works in the UK as an illustrator and creative designer, accompanied by her beloved pets. Elisa loves quietness and feels truly at home in nature.